BRITAIN IN OLD PHOTOGRAPHS

AROUND RIPLEY

J U L I E   P O T T O N   &   J A N E T   N O R T H

J.Potton

J North

ALAN SUTTON PUBLISHING LIMITED

In collaboration with
Derbyshire County Council

Alan Sutton Publishing Limited
Phoenix Mill · Far Thrupp · Stroud
Gloucestershire · GL5 2BU

DERBYSHIRE
County Council
We're proud of Derbyshire.

First published 1995

Cover photographs: (front) John Wheeldon, ratcatcher; (back) miners in Pentrich Colliery, 1895.

British Library Cataloguing in Publication Data.
A catalogue record for this book is available from the British Library.

ISBN 0-7509-0938-2

Typeset in 9/10 Sabon.
Typesetting and origination by
Alan Sutton Publishing Limited.
Printed in Great Britain by
WBC Ltd, Bridgend, Glamorgan.

Mr Arthur Taylor. Local tradition has it that his father created a drink which later became the famous Coca-Cola. He wasn't successful in Britain, and so emigrated to America. The makers of Coca-Cola today, however, do not seem to know of this possible connection.

Contents

Acknowledgements

The photographs used in this book are part of the Len Wood Collection held at Ripley Library; Derbyshire Library Service has kindly consented to their use in this publication. Every effort has been made to acknowledge and trace possible interested parties, and to attribute correctly names, dates, places and information. However, Len has left us with an incomplete written record of his collection, and Derbyshire Library Service continues to work on the identification and cataloguing of the many hundreds of images bequeathed to it. The authors would therefore be grateful to hear about any errors or omissions that may have occurred in the writing of this book, and would be pleased to receive further information about the photographs included. Amendments and additional acknowledgements will be made in future editions, and the details added permanently to Ripley Library's catalogue of the Len Wood Collection for the information of future generations.

Ripley Library already has a very large and well-used collection of photographs covering the Ripley, Codnor, Denby and Heage area. However there is always room for addition and expansion. Staff would be most interested to see any other photographs or local items you may have. Staff at any Derbyshire public library would also be happy to receive photographs of their area as donations or loans for copying.

Albert Taylor of Waingroves and his horse.

Introduction

In a newspaper article of 1988 Len Wood said he had always wanted to compile his own book of photographs, made up of 'Then and Now' scenes. Although we could not accommodate all of these within the current project, this book is dedicated to his memory.

Len and his wife Adah lived, for most of their lives, near the Iron Bridge on Nottingham Road, Ripley. At the age of fourteen, armed with a plate camera, Len started on a hobby which was to become a lifetime interest. He was keen to amass a comprehensive collection of photographs for future generations to use; and so he began to acquire pictures from family, friends and acquaintances, although details of his sources are now unknown. For the most part, however, he and his wife cycled around Derbyshire photographing items of interest. It is not unusual to see their bicycles on the corner of a photograph, or even occasionally Adah herself. Such was his local standing, that whenever a building was to be demolished or altered, the Council would notify Len, in order that he record it for posterity.

Not content with photography, however, Len also took great pleasure in giving talks about the history of the area to local organizations; these included slide shows. He also contributed many articles to the local weekly newspaper, the *Ripley and Heanor News*; these were often 'Then and Now' scenes to show the changing face of the town. Some of his photographs were also loaned for use in local history books such as Fred Thorpe's *History of Codnor and Loscoe*, and several appear in booklets by the Heanor Historical Society. Although largely of the Ripley and Heanor areas there are also items from further afield, even from outside Derbyshire. Len Wood was also interested in silent films and had an impressive collection.

When he died in January 1992, Len's photographic collection was passed over to Ripley Library as he bequeathed, and it is still there for public consultation. Since this time the library staff have been sorting and cataloguing it for future use. A great deal of work has already been carried out on the collection, but much still remains to be done. It currently amounts to over 1,500 prints of old and new images of the area, and a future project will be to sort the many slides used in his talks. The captions and information used with the photographs throughout this book have been largely supplied by Len, although occasionally some alteration or verification has been necessary.

Knowing how important the collection is to the people of Ripley, Derbyshire Library Service has made every effort to promote and use the images currently available. To date there have been various exhibitions held in Ripley Library, and several books of photographs have been produced using some of the images. It is hoped to continue using the collection in similar ways in the future.

The book is intended not only as a tribute to one man's perseverance and dedication to a subject in which he was passionately interested, but also stands as a reminder of buildings, streets and a way of life, past and present, in the Ripley area.

Railway workers at Hammersmith accompanied by Len Wood on the right. The chimney in the background was demolished, brick by brick, in October 1978.

The Horse and Groom public house on Oxford Street. It closed in 1980 and was subsequently converted into the current Yorkshire Bank premises.

Section One

AROUND RIPLEY

Ripley town centre, c. 1908. This view was taken from the water tower, before Shirley Road School and Crossley Park were established. Ogle's Works, the Town Hall and the Co-op buildings can be identified, and in the far distance to the left is Swanwick Church.

The Market Place, focal point of the town centre. These two photographs show some of the changes. The frontage of the Town Hall has not changed much in recent years: on the earlier photo of 1906, above, it has no additional low building; while the later photo of 1948 shows a long low structure, which was a bus shelter. In the background can be seen two of the three 'faces' of the Red Lion pub. In one it is thatched, and the second shows it with a tiled roof. It was later rebuilt in its present form following a road accident which partly demolished it. The building has not been used as a pub since 1990.

Taken from the Town Hall, this view of the Market Place in 1906 shows the old elm tree outside the Thorn Tree pub. Over the years there has been some discussion as to whether the tree was an elm or a thorn. It was sawn down in 1910 but its main claim to fame is that it was believed to be the place where John Wesley preached on his visit to Ripley.

A view back down High Street, showing the Red Lion when it was thatched. On the left of the photo a clock can be seen. It has since disappeared, but originally marked the position of the post office, which opened in 1857. The post master was James Warrener. It later became Brentnall's estate agents.

High Street, *c.* 1906.

High Street, *c.* 1912. Horse fairs were regular events in several local towns, including Ripley. The Ripley fair was reputedly famous for its young horses.

This relatively modern view of High Street shows some of the changes since 1906. Rowells is now Boots the Chemists, and Hursts have recently modernised their shop front. More significant is 'Rowells Clock', which was bought by Mr Godkin in 1980 and repositioned above Boole's newsagents, where it still hangs. It was a favourite local landmark for courting couples to meet under, in days gone by.

Oxford Street, *c.* 1919. Hursts is now on the left-hand corner and Amanda Generations on the right.

Church Street, 1908. J.S. Reynolds on the left corner is now Godkins newsagents.

The opposite side of Church Street, 1912. A card shop and Ladbroke's bookmakers now occupy two of these shops.

Looking back up Church Street, *c.* 1953. The houses on the left were knocked down in 1963. A Mr Norman ran an undertaking service in one of the buildings. Cash's solicitors offices were above the self-service store further up the street and also stretched into the upper part of the house

Grove Villa, *c.* 1920. This formed a part of the houses through the gate in the above photo. It backed on to Cash's office buildings.

Church Street, 1979. These buildings are on the site of Grove Villa and the other demolished houses shown in the earlier Church Street photographs. The Card Box has since been converted into a ground floor entrance for Hardy, Miles and Titterton solicitors. The shops opposite the church are also newly rebuilt.

Looking up Church Street, 1970s. Burton Tailoring is now Spondon Motor Spares and Woolworths has closed, allowing Amber Value to extend into larger premises.

The Ripley Co-op fish and meat department shop, Grosvenor Road. This is now the site of Chasers wine bar.

Cope's House, Grosvenor Road, 1971. Occupied by Lee, Son and Cope auctioneers, this one-time chapel was next door to the current library buildings.

Co-op Square. Several now demolished buildings are worth noting. The white building on the left in the far distance was the Co-op shoe repair shop and next to it, at the side of the Electra Theatre, was Couch's sweet shop. On the right of the photograph is the chapel manse, which has been converted into shops. The site is currently occupied by a funeral parlour and a financial adviser.

A later view of Co-op Square taken from the opposite end. It shows the Ebenezer Chapel, which was home to Ripley Library for many years. The chapel was demolished in 1974 and became a car park.

Co-op Square, taken from Nottingham Road, *c.* 1920. Mr George Golding is standing in his doorway to the front right. He was a keen photographer.

Greenwich, Nottingham Road, *c.* 1915. Notice the tramlines. Known locally as the 'Ripley Rattlers', trams ran between Ripley and Nottingham from 1913 to 1932.

A field walk from Cromford Road down old Hartshay Hill, *c.* 1906. On the left now is Amber Heights and on the right is the Lons Estate.

Jockey Row, Cromford Road. This was knocked down in 1967. The Horse and Jockey was set back from the road until the new Hartshay Hill was made.

The Beeches, Cromford Road, 1920s. It was opposite the Kenning's tyre depot which later became individual factory units.

The bandstand in Crossley Park. The nearby water tower was demolished in 1967.

John Wood, landlord of the Albion Inn, Butterley Hill, shown with his donkey and cart, *c.* 1910. Local youngsters were renowned for sneaking rides on the donkey, who, when not pulling the cart, lived in the field behind the inn. The lady on the left is Miss Bassett, a former barmaid. The Albion closed in 1979 and has since been converted into a private house.

Ripley Co-op's first store, which was next to the Greyhound Inn on Butterley Hill. The house still stands but the sign has vanished.

The old Coach Road, Butterley Plain.

Derby Road, *c.* 1900. St John's Church is on the right. Although the church still stands, it is now 'The Spring of Living Waters Church'.

The old chapel on Derby Road, Marehay. It later became the site for the Kingdom Hall for Jehovah's Witnesses.

The Windmill pub, Steam Mill Lane. Adah Wood is standing outside. The pub was demolished owing to mining subsidence. Houses now stand on the site.

Wright's Farm, *c.* 1937. When this was demolished, it became the site for William Birk's old people's flats on the Porterhouse Estate.

A distant view of Hall's Farm, *c.* 1945. The housing estate now to the right had not yet been built.

Hall's Farm, Steam Mill Lane, *c.* 1908. At the back of the farm was extensive stabling for the Ripley Colliery ponies.

An interesting view of the Loades match factory on Steam Mill Lane, taken from the old railway bank. The business started in 1926 using match splints and ready-made matchboxes, imported from Russia. It was known as the Triumph Match Factory and at its peak employed twenty people. However, on 30 September 1929 there was a fire, and the company was subsequently bought out by the British Match Corporation.

A picture of the matchbox. It was known as the Derby match because the local town was Derby, but the horse and jockey motif was chosen to depict the famous 'Derby' horse race. The covers were printed by Brittain and Sons Ltd.

Eyres Lane, *c*. 1937. This was at the back of Codnor Gate Farm and led to Forty Horse Fields. It is now a part of Codnor Industrial Estate.

Codnor Gate Farm, owned by the Lynams.

BUTTERLEY
COMPANY

Butterley Company was founded in 1790 by Benjamin Outram, William Jessop, Francis Beresford and John Wright. It is one of the oldest iron founders in Britain. This shows the entrance to Butterley works, which still remains largely unchanged. A post office can be seen on the left; at some stage it had also been situated in the octagonal building to the right. Underneath here the company fire brigade garaged their engine.

The Butterley horse-drawn fire engine, 1903. The driver was Samuel Goodall, who worked at Butterley Company, and the captain was Arthur Gibson. They are pictured outside the station which was situated at the bottom of Butterley Hill.

Butterley Fire Company. From left to right: Mr W. Foster (vice captain), A. Gibson (captain), J. Attewell (driver), Chris Gibson, C. Hague, R. Mansey, C. Hardwick, G. Gibson, W. Cheetham, S. Clarke.

Assembled foremen from the Bridge Yard, *c.* 1900. The gentleman seated on the right is Frank Anthoney.

Butterley machine shop workers, 1936.

Foundry workers.

Jack Cupits' railway gang. Left to right: Arthur Sutcliff, Doug Morrell, Jack Watchorn, Jack Cupit (foreman).

A long service presentation at Butterley Company Ltd. Back row, left to right: Arthur Barlow, -?-, Jack King, Ambrose Grimshaw, Alan Herbert, Tom Bradshaw, Ray Seeds, Len Bradley, Charlie Rick. Middle row: Len Wood, -?-, Sid Vardy, Sid Wood, Arthur Gibson, Chris Walters, Stanley Ottewell, Albert Woodward, Bill Hardwick, George Morrell, Anthony Buckley, Jack Groom, -?-, Cyril Clark. Front row: Harry Muggeridge, Arthur College, Ken Holland, -?-, Alf Cook, Bill Roberts, Eddy Hartington.

The building of the pattern shop
on Cinder Bank, Hammersmith.

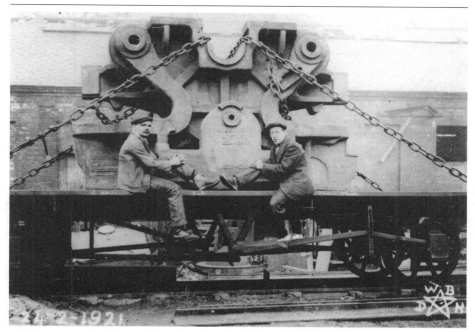

Alf Parker to the left and Douglas Hornbuckle on the right, 24 February 1921. This propeller shaft bearing was made for a large liner at Butterley.

The Butterley Bridge Yard group with the completed Kafr-el-Zayat bridge, made for the Egyptian state railways, November 1947.

The building of St Pancras station roof, 1867. It was designed by John Alleyne, and at 240 ft it was the largest roof span in the world at that time. It is a tied arch with no supports; the ties run underneath the platforms and rails. A plaque on the station wall still commemorates this feat.

ALL IN A DAY'S
WORK

Bonsall's saddler's shop situated on Derby Road near to St John's School.

Sid Street's butcher's shop, which stood between the Three Horse Shoes and White Lion inns. Sid Street moved from Belper to Ripley in 1910. As well as running a shop, he served on Ripley Urban District Council for eleven years. He died in 1977, aged ninety-two. His other achievement was to hold a driving licence from 1914, with no driving offences.

Sid, or Charles Sidney, moved to the Market Place in about 1919, running a fish and chip business until he retired. This shop later changed hands to become a shop for bankrupt stock, before being demolished to make way for the new council offices. During foundation work on the new building a coal seam was found, a reflection of Ripley's mining roots.

The Co-op provision and butchers stores. The Co-op took up butchery seriously in 1877, but had been dealing in pork as early as 1864. In 1879 the provisions and butchery departments combined.

Horse-drawn drays, c. 1912. Used for deliveries by the Co-op, they were kept in Booth Street Yard.

F. P. MILLS,

ENGLISH FAMILY BUTCHER,

Also States Chilled Beef and Colonial Meat Purveyor.

CANTERBURY LAMB A SPECIALITY.
PICKLED TONGUES.

F.P.M. wishes it to be distinctly understood that the English Trade is conducted on one side of the Shop only and guarantees that every person is served with the class of Meat asked for, for which he holds himself entirely responsible.

Best Quality of Meat in all Branches kept at Lowest Possible Prices.

NOTE THE ADDRESS

Church St., : RIPLEY.

Randolph C. Nield, Photo.

This advertisement for Mills butchers of Church Street contains an interesting reference to 'purveyor of colonial meat'.

A joint advertisement from 1927, showing various services on offer. At least two of these advertisements indicate that Ripley had its fair share of wealthy people, complete with servants.

Two more advertisements from 1927. At one time the post office was in the Red Lion pub. Unfortunately, although Ellisons had been established for twenty-five years, they are not in business today.

One business that did not fare so well, however, was the Ripley Manufacturing Company, which produced textiles. On Monday 11 June 1923 fire gutted the 1,166 square yards of offices, causing £50,000 worth of damage. The aftermath can be seen here.

The Manufacturing Company chimney being demolished, November 1973. This was situated on Wellington Street/Crossley Street.

Birks Farm, situated at the top of Hill Street, off Butterley Hill, *c.* 1916. When the buildings fell into disrepair they were demolished and new houses erected.

Outside Birks Farm, *c.* 1909. The little girl is Minnie Clark, later Mrs Harry Stanley of Riddings.

The Birks family by the side of their haystack, *c.* 1902. Left to right: Jane, Hetty, Sam, Elizabeth, Ellen and head of the family, Samuel. Standing on the ladder is Frederick and still hard at work on top is William, or Edmund as he was also known.

A distant view of Pentrich Colliery. First opened in the 1840s, it was one of Derbyshire's oldest pits. It was also one of the first Ripley pits to use automatic coal cutters. Although it backed on to Butterley-owned pits, it remained private until its closure in 1944.

A closer view of Pentrich Colliery, 12 September 1934. In the background the railway viaduct can be seen. Pit ponies were removed in 1934, and according to a newspaper article of the time, Pentrich was the first Derbyshire pit to dispense with them entirely.

Miners at work underground in Pentrich Colliery, 1 April 1895. It is rare to find photographs of underground life in a colliery. This is partly because of the exposure time needed to take the photograph. The result was sometimes a ghost, as can be seen in the picture below.

This picture of an engine also dates from 1 April 1895.

There were plenty of jobs above ground as well. This group of men worked at Pentrich's fitting stub shop; the photograph dates from 12 November 1904.

A distant view of Ripley Colliery, one of Butterley Company's pits. It opened in about 1863 and merged with Denby Hall in 1949.

The headstock at Ripley Colliery.

Two more Butterley Company pits. Bailey Brook Colliery was also known as Heanor Colliery. There was a name change in 1832 to Langley Colliery but it was always more commonly known as Bailey Brook. The pit closed in 1938.

Ormonde Colliery, near Loscoe, c. 1904. It closed in September 1970.

Denby Hall Colliery, another Butterley Company pit. It eventually closed in 1968.

An interesting early view of Denby Pottery, *c.* 1933. The company was founded by Joseph Bourne in 1809. Early products were salt-glazed bottles and jars. The site looks very different today; there is a distinct lack of chimneys, and the dirt track is now a busy road.

Two scenes, 4 September 1931. They show flooding around the railway line at Sawmills, Ambergate, and boys sitting out of the way of flood water at Stevensons Dye works.

Crich Quarry workmen.

An unidentified group of sawmillers at an unknown location.

Section Four

HIGH DAYS AND
HOLIDAYS

This service was to commemorate the laying of the foundation stone for St Joseph's

Church, Butterley Hill, 28 May 1930. The Bishop of Nottingham, the Right Revd

Thomas Dunn laid the stone. The parish priest was Revd Father J.B. Farmer. The

inscription read 'AMDG et in honorem Sti Joseph lapidem posruit Thomas Epus

Nottinghamensis. Dic XXVlll, Maii, AD MCMXXX'. *The church officially*

opened in December 1930, having been built by Carney and Son of Derby at a cost of

£2,300. Before this the congregation had worshipped at Butterley Grange Chapel and

later in a room adjoining the Rose and Crown.

The coronation parade for King George V and Queen Mary, Glasshouse Hill, Codnor, 1911.

Bonfires were often built to celebrate such occasions. It is believed that the bonfire on the left was made by Butterley Company in 1902 as 'a peace and Coronation bonfire' and erected at High Holborn, Codnor. It was lit by Fitzherbert Wright of Butterley Company. He was also High Sheriff of Derbyshire. The bonfire on the right was on Monument Hill, Codnor, in 1911. Both must have made impressive sights, being visible for miles around once lit.

The Ripley Company of the 5th Notts and Derby Regiment of the Sherwood Foresters, 4 August 1914, seen here marching across the Market Place after starting from the Drill Hall on Shirley Road. They marched to Derby to join their battalion. Their commander was Captain Fryar, son of Mark Fryar of Denby, accompanied by Regimental Sergeant Major Newcomb. The term of service was for three years or as long as the war lasted, and each man received cigarettes and a good luck card from G.C. Brittain.

Celebration on the Market Place to mark the end of the First World War.

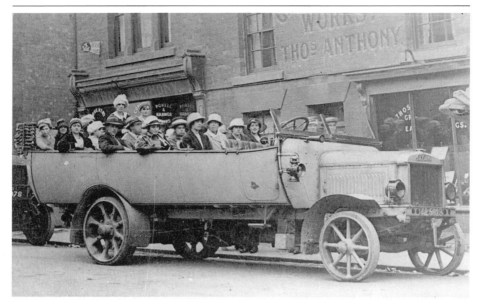

Outings were usually a treat, and few and far between. Charabancs were often used, and several companies in Ripley operated services. This trip started from outside Greenwich Cycle Works on Co-op Square.

Beighton Street, *c*. 1918. This charabanc trip started from the end of Beighton Street.

The Smithams on a trip to Via Gellia, 1904. This pony and trap was another mode of transport belonging to this well-known Ripley family. Included are Mr and Mrs Smitham, Mabel, Rene, Walter, Grandma Smitham and Grandma Fowler.

Allsopp's brake is seen here leaving Co-op Square for Matlock, *c.* 1912. The building behind the brake is the current National Westminster Bank.

Although the occasion and date are not known for this gathering, several people have been identified on it. In the back row are Mrs Priestley, Mrs Lynam of Codnor Gate Farm, Mrs Beech, who lived next door to Len Wood, and Maria Briggs of Ryknield Road, Kilburn. In the middle row is Mrs Large, who owned a smallholding near Iron Bridge. If nothing more, it is indicative of an age when group photographs were taken on an outing. This sadly is often not the case today.

The Mount Tabor Church outing to Sherwood Forest, *c.* 1909. Mount Tabor was the Methodist chapel at the top of Argyll Road, now an antique shop. Back row, left to right: Arthur Crooks, Jack Crooks, Mr Needham, Charlie Woolley, Mr Seals (choirmaster), Mr Pickard (grandfather of tennis coach Tony Pickard), Mr Woolley, Mr Lynam, Harry Foster, George Taylor, Jack Woolley. Third row: Mrs Brown, Mrs Needham, Mr and Mrs Crooks, Leslie Henshaw, Josiah Brown, Jack Lynam, Reg Taylor, Mrs Taylor, Miss Fowler (organist), Mrs Jones, Mr Henshaw (Sunday school superintendent and New Denby Colliery manager). Second row: Lily Seals, Rose Jones, Alice Woolley, Mrs Woolley, Alice Marsh, Esther Johnson, Annie Fowler, Miss Jones. Front row: Mr Brown, Albert Fowler, Jessie Fowler, Lily Crooks, Maggie Woolley, Laura Brown, Elsie Anthony, Kathleen and Cedric Taylor.

The Nottingham Road Primitive Methodists, 1909. A yearly event was the Sunday school walk by the local chapels. This was normally on Whit Monday and involved a walk from Ripley to Codnor Park Monument.

Walking along Chapel Street, Codnor, on another Sunday school walk. The men and the women walk in separate lines.

Ripley Carnival, outside the Town Hall, 1932. The queen was Nancy Marshall, Bert Weekly king and Mr Cuttell the jester. The train bearers were Peter Cash and Kathleen Standing.

The same group can be seen here at Ripley station. They arrived by train and specials were laid on for those travelling from further afield. Among the maids of honour were Vera Langton, Evelyn Morrell, Florence Woodward, Brydd Alton and Lily Williamson.

No carnival would be complete without floats. The photographs are thought to date from the 1930s. Note that the Red Lion does not have a thatched roof.

The Fair, 1908. This has always been held in October, as laid down in the charter granted to the town in 1215. It is always a smaller part of the Nottingham Goose Fair.

A Bradford-based engine called the *I Wonder*, which visited the fair every year. Albert Barker, owner of the vehicle, is the man on the left. The Thompson van in the background belonged to a Ripley family who were based at the bottom of Outram Street.

Street parties and gatherings have often been held for all sorts of events. These people are standing on Mill Lane, Codnor, but the reason and date are unknown.

Celebrating the Victory Day Parade, 1919. A gathering outside the Lord Byron and Miners Arms pubs on the corner of Wright Street and Mill Lane, Codnor.

Ripley Scouts on parade at the corner of Wood Street and Moseley Street, *c.* 1920.

The 'Son of Kong' float by Ripley Scouts first made its appearance in the 1934 carnival. It was 14 ft 2 in high and 7 ft 6 in wide. They didn't win a prize, but so popular was their entry that Billy Butlin later heard of it and asked them to lead the procession at Skegness carnival, which they did. Unfortunately, Kong got damp over the ensuing winter and so it was decided to burn him on Forty Horse Silver Jubilee beacon bonfire on 6 May 1935.

Ripley's United Silver Prize Band. In 1922 and 1923 they won the Crystal Palace shield, and to that date, had won seventeen first prizes, eleven seconds, three thirds and twenty special events.

Codnor Band, *c.* 1906. The band was founded in 1860.

Ripley Kiltie Carnival band marching along Nottingham Road.

Eddie Cresswell, drum major with the Kilties.

It is not unusual for public houses to be the venue for various social clubs and activities. The Albion Inn on Butterley Hill was no exception. Although the nature of this gathering is unknown, the Butterley Male Voice Glee Club met here in about 1914. The landlord, John Wood, is standing underneath the lamp in the centre of the photo.

ENTERTAINMENT AND SPORT

One form of entertainment was to make your own.
This advertisement from 1927 reflects the interests
and needs of an era since vanished. It is also
interesting to note the address, Tram Terminus.

The Hippodrome, 1954. It was built by John Marshall and opened on 28 July 1913. It was once home to operatic performances as well as operating as a cinema. The frontage today remains largely unchanged.

The Hippodrome orchestra, used in the days of silent film, *c*. 1919. From left to right: Mr West, Mr Dilks, Mr Oakley, Mr Henshaw, Mr Holmes and Mr Lloyd.

Although this photograph of the Electra Theatre (taken in 1910) has been reproduced on many occasions, it is particularly pertinent to the memory of Len Wood. All the people in the picture are related to him. His grandfather, Sam Hornbuckle, was commissionaire, his grandmother a cleaner, his uncle Arthur a projectionist, and his two aunts worked inside.

Mr Norman Gray was the first resident manager of the Electra, *c.* 1919.

This photograph is of the programme cover from the 1913 film of *Les Miserables*. It was shown at the Empire Palace. An original copy of the programme can be found at Ripley Library. A silent film, it featured French actors, most notable of whom was Mistinguett, who later starred at the *Folies Bergère*.

A film advertisement, probably for the Empire. *Through the Back Door* was made in 1921.

The filming of Howard Spring's novel *The Shabby Tiger* at Crich Tramway Museum, 1973.

Eric Grainger was a miner from Codnor, who took up professional boxing between the wars. Like most boxers of his time, he did a day's work down the pit and then in the evening had a ten-round boxing match which, if successful, earned him £5. He started boxing at the age of fifteen, training with the Mellor brothers and Bill Gordon of Codnor. His first fight was in Stewart's boxing booth during Ripley Fair against Sam Minto; six rounds earned him £1. After this he registered as a professional with Charlie Coates of Sutton in Ashfield. In 1936 he knocked out Gunner Thomson and Kid Haycox, which gained him the Midlands Counties Lightweight and Welterweight titles. In total he had sixty fights in halls, losing only eight, and a further eight seasons in boxing booths travelling around the country. In winter he continued to work the pits.

Like Eric Grainger, Percy Illsley was for a time a miner, but was also a successful amateur wrestler. He was born in 1893 in Ripley and died in 1977, aged eighty-four. His wife Minnie is believed to be the oldest resident in Ripley and recently opened the new Ripley and District Heritage Centre.

There have been several football teams in Ripley. This shows the Wesleyan club in the 1927/28 season.

Another picture of a Ripley football team, this time undated.

The Ripley Junior football club during their 1927/28 season. Back row, left to right: G. Curzon, C. Briggs, R.W. Claxton (secretary), R. Bamford, F. Cuttel, E. Grainger, H. Parkin, J. Jones, J. Stone, J. Evans (trainer) -?-. Front row: L. Cuttel, J. Lynam, A. Curzon, H. Reynolds, W. Seal.

Pinxton Boat Rangers of the Boat Inn during the 1908/09 season. They were the Bulwell and District League champions.

Another sport played in many towns and villages was cricket. Here is the Codnor Miners' Welfare team during the 1927/28 season.

Codnor Miners' Welfare again, this time in 1930.

Butterley cricket club, first eleven. In 1906 they were champions of the Derbyshire Senior Alliance. Those in the picture include W.H. Blount (secretary), W. Hogg, J. Disney (captain), H. Walters, G. Burgin, G. Fowler, J. Moon, J. Farnsworth, H. Statham, W. Watson, A. Hogg, W. Foster, W. Cresswell and F. Slater.

When you haven't got a sports or leisure centre, you have to find another venue for your swimming gala. Brickyard Pond near the Porterhouse estate was just such a site. As can be seen from these photographs, at least one swimming gala was held here. Sadly the pond has since been filled in.

This early photo of another swimming event has not been recognised or dated. However, it is indicative of a style which has since disappeared.

Cycling races through the town are not uncommon. The Milk Race has passed through on more than one occasion. This event has not been identified, but took place in 1974. By now the Iron Bridge has been pulled down, but pre-dates the development of the Codnor Industrial Estate. The grassy field is now a car dealer's showroom. Len Wood lived on the opposite side of the road, a little further down.

Greenwich Cycle Works, situated just off Co-op Square, and now the site of Crest of the Wave. It was at this time owned and run by Thomas Anthony & Co. In one of their advertisements they described their wares as 'incandescent goods of the best quality'. It is also interesting to note that, as well as cycles, they sold air rifles and other sporting goods.

CHILDHOOD – THE BEST YEARS OF ONE'S LIFE

*This picture probably shows the sum total of the pupils at Horsley School because it is a
mixed photograph of boys and girls. The date and names of the children are unknown.*

Ripley Council School, which was situated on Shirley Road. When the school moved to its current location, the buildings were demolished and the site is now a housing estate. Unfortunately, neither photo is dated.

Schoolchildren at Denby Free School.

The Church School, Crosshill, Codnor, 1906. This school was erected in 1844 and was initially mixed. In 1895 it became a boys' school. The building was demolished in the 1970s.

Crich Scouts marching down the main street, 1920s.

TRANSPORT

The arrival of Ripley's first steam roller in 1896 must have been an exciting and unusual event. Members of the Urban District Council turned out. Left to right: A. Walters, John Fletcher, R. Argile, A. Arthur, C. Lawton, G. Key, George Capon (clerk), S. Stanley, W.B. Bembridge, M. Hooper, S. Fletcher, T. Cutts (rate collector), James Crossley, T. Hanlon, John Moss and C. Sheton (inspector of nuisances). At the wheel was Thomas Kemp the surveyor. Rumour has it that as the steam roller was brought from Butterley; one of the above members walked in front, clearing the road of stones and debris. In the background is Moss's pork butchers, later Boots the Chemist and more recently Amber Valley Planning offices.

Widening the railway bridge on Nottingham Road, ready for trams, 1913.

Ripley's first tram as it leaves the tram terminus in Co-op Square, 1913. D.H. Lawrence wrote a short story based on this journey entitled *Tickets Please*. This could have been based on personal research, as he had relatives in Ripley.

By 1920 trams were well established. This one is on its way from Co-op Square.

Trams travelled through Codnor on their way to Nottingham. This picture was taken some time between 1914 and 1918 at Crosshill station.

In 1925 the LMS line was used as a testing ground for the Sentinel Cammell Laird steam rail coach. Here it can be seen entering Ripley station. It had a locomotive and two carriages, and carried fifty-six passengers plus luggage. It could also be driven from either end. At 16 tons unloaded, it was 80 per cent lighter than ordinary branch line trains, and the coal consumption was 75 per cent less than a normal train. Was this an early forerunner of the Sprinter train now in operation on many smaller lines?

A view from the Nottingham Road bridge, down on to the Ripley station warehouse. This has since been demolished.

Ripley station opened on 1 October 1889 and closed in 1963. It was then used by Clower's builders merchants for a while as a storage unit. However, in 1985 when they reorganised it was decided to demolish it, and the Midland Railway Trust handled the demolition.

Butterley station, 1917.

A train passing through Butterley.

Crosshill station, Codnor, 1912. The stationmaster on the left of the bottom photo is Mr Bartholomew, and Mr Freeman is on the right. The station opened in June 1890 and closed in 1926. It was on the Heanor and Pye Bridge branch of the Midland Railway.

When the railway line finally closed, there was no need for the bridge at Crosshill, but the road had to be widened for cars. Here the bridge is being demolished and the line filled in. Widening took place in March 1955.

Denby station, Street Lane, Denby, *c.* 1910.

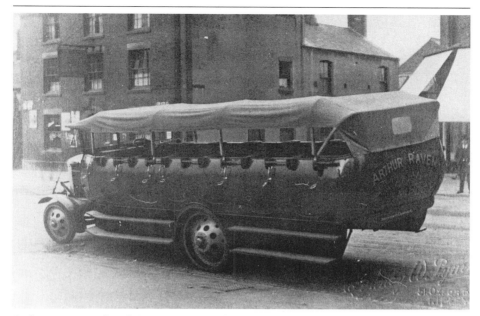

Arthur Raven's charabancs, *c.* 1921. The two vehicles were kept in a large wooden garage in the Thorn Tree pub yard. The conductor stood on the running board of one vehicle to collect fares. Both had benches that ran the length of the charas while passengers entered via individual doors.

Codnor's first motor car, a De Dion Bouton, which was owned by Dr George Thomson. Dr Thomson came to Codnor in 1901 and retired in 1945. This occasion was a tree planting to commemorate the coronation of George V. Dr Thomson is at the wheel with C.W. Ridyard by his side. The other passengers were Mrs Ridyard, Mrs G. Thomson, Mrs Eyre, Vera Ridyard and Keith Thomson.

Looking up towards the Iron Bridge
on Nottingham Road from Steam
Mill Lane, *c.* 1920. A tram and
Williamson's bus are passing.

The last days of the trolley bus, 1953. The overhead wires are being removed.

The Iron Bridge on Nottingham Road. A mineral line ran from Brittain's Colliery across the bridge. Once the colliery closed there was no use for the bridge. It was demolished on 27 April 1969.

A sketch by an unknown artist showing the railway bridge at Buckland Hollow, which has since been demolished.

Butterley tunnel was originally 2,966 yards long, but was later extended to 3,063 yards. Although it still exists, it finally closed in 1900 when it was no longer considered safe. As with many canal tunnels, it is so narrow and long that the only way to pass through it was by 'legging'. This took six hours, and as this sketch of 1845, by Thomas Frost shows, it took two men, one on either side of the boat.

Taken in 1980 on Lowes Hill, this photograph shows Adah Wood standing at the point where the layout of the existing road and hill had to be changed to accommodate the A610 link road.

Constructing the new bypass, the A61, October 1976.

Section Eight

PEOPLE

*Alec Lamb, a well-known local character from
Codnor, c. 1900. He sold firewood and delivered
newspapers.*

Mr Shipman of Ripley. When he was a
hundred years old, he was taken for a ride
around the town by horse and trap.

The late Dr Howse of Horsley Woodhouse.

John Wheeldon, better known as John Gaunt. He lived at Sawmills but worked for the Midland Railway Company, travelling the lines as a ratcatcher. He is the only person known to have successfully trained foxes to 'rat' for economic use, and claimed they were better than terriers because they could hold five rats in their mouths at once. The ratcatcher had to be quick because, unlike a terrier, foxes did not kill the rats outright. His best two foxes, however, were killed accidentally by gamekeepers. Such was his national fame that he was described in a book as a 'great sportsman and great Englishman'. He died, aged seventy-three, at the home of a friend in Belper in November 1924, and was buried in Crich churchyard.

The names and fate of these Belgian refugees are unknown.

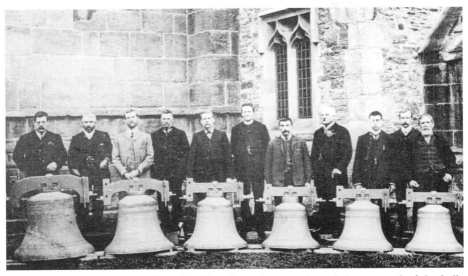

Various church dignitaries of Denby Church on the occasion of the removal of the bells for repairs and tuning in 1907. Left to right: Francis Weston (bell ringer), Alfred Orme (sexton), William Briggs (bell ringer), John Cresswell (churchwarden), Elijah Briggs (bell ringer), the Revd Mr F.S. Boissier, Albert Cresswell (bell ringer), John Simkiss, (churchwarden) Percy Weston (bell ringer), Uriah Hunt (organist), Matthew Cresswell (bell ringer).

The Ambergate Cottage Garden Society, 1920s. Back row, left to right: Mr Williams, Mr Cowlishaw, Mr Lloyd, Mr Forthan (Heage UDC surveyor), Mr Holliday. Third row: Mr Drake, J. Clough, J. Woodhead, J. Stone, J. Green, Albert Wilkins. Second row: B. Glossop (with bicycle), John Jessop, John Gaunt (Midland Railway ratcatcher), Edwin Glossop (owner of Ambergate brickworks), H. Redfern, George Holmes, J. Bonnell (painter and decorator), J. Cooper, J. Key, W. Ray (with bicycle). The front row includes: W. Oldfield, J. Butterworth, A. Watherston (headmaster of Ambergate School), A. Kay (manager of Ambergate brickworks), George Fearn, Mr Collington.

The Bethel Sunday School young men's class of 1905. Back row, left to right: Wilfred Loades, Kalen Ford, Albert Loades, Les Cresswell, Herbert Loades, Percy Cresswell, Mr Statham. Middle row: Leonard Bonsall, Andrew Hatfield, Tom Hatfield, Bill Johnson, Harold Bonsall, Will Bonsall, Mr Whitehouse, Charles Fairbrother, Fred Holloway, Frank Holloway, Mr Ludlam. Front row: -?-, Tom Taylor, Tom Godkin, Richard Marriott, George White, Tom Ludlam, Bill Oldfield, -?-.

LOCAL LANDMARKS

The Steam Mill, Steam Mill Lane. The building had stood for over 200 years before being demolished in the early 1900s. Together with the windmill situated further up the road, the two buildings were owned by the Steeples family of Codnor from the nineteenth century. Latterly Wilfred Steeples owned them. He was the nephew of Albert Loades, owner of the nearby match factory.

A distant view over Hammersmith, showing the famed and unusual double bridge in the distance to the left of the photograph.

The double bridge, which was taken down in 1976 to make way for the bypass. The top part had two railway lines running over it; one was the main line, and the other the mineral line from Brittain Pit to Butterley Company. The bottom part of the bridge spanned a footpath to Cromford Canal. This still remains but has been filled in.

Waingroves Hall, built between 1671 and 1680 by Richard Clayton, son of Richard Clayton of Codnor Breach. It was remodelled between 1790 and 1800. The top floor windows are decorated with the Strelley Arms after Robert Strelley of Oakerthorpe, who undertook the final rebuilding. By the 1860s it had become a tenanted farm before being bought by Captain T.G. Laurie MC, during the war. In 1982 it was sold for about £68,000.

Codnor Park Monument, c. 1908. This monument was erected in 1854 in memoriam to William Jessop Jnr. Mr Jessop was one of the founders of Butterley Company, particularly associated with the construction of the Cromford Canal. On this occasion it was the venue for the annual Whit Monday Sunday school outing.

Three views of Codnor Castle. The castle was originally believed to be a motte and bailey, built in the twelfth century for the de Codnor family. It was never really a castle but more a fortified manor house of three storeys. The second Lord Grey extended the house to form a Lower Court, with circular towers and turrets. The Upper Court was used as living quarters. In 1496 it passed to the Zouches. In 1634 it was bought by Dr Richard Neill, Archbishop of York, who built a farmhouse on the east side, using castle stone. In the 1860s it was sold to Butterley Company and in 1978 to the National Coal Board.

Before and after shots of the castle, showing the collapse of a major piece of walling. The first was taken in 1906, with the wall to the left intact; the second was after the collapse in 1909. Dismantling of stone started as early as 1648 and the stone used to build local farmhouses, including Home Farm on Alfreton Road and a cottage on Nottingham Road.

Two external views of Codnor Dovecote. This was in the grounds of Codnor Castle and is said to have been at least 500 years old. The first photograph was taken in 1938. The second must have been taken later because of the increased disrepair of the structure. It was finally demolished in 1969.

An internal view of the dovecote. The walls were 5 ft thick and 22 ft high. The entrance was 3 ft 6 in wide. There were twenty rows of nest holes holding up to four hundred birds. Some restoration work was carried out in 1904.

......dest ..ouse, situated on Nottingham Road, was built in 1649. On the roof .... the unusual sundial pictured in the photograph below. This has since ....d with a replica to preserve the original from further erosion.

Fritchley Windmill, *c.* 1880.

Heage Windmill, also known locally as Ned's Mill. It ceased working in about 1918. In 1966 it received a Building Preservation Order and the County Council subsequently bought it. In the early 1970s it was then restored to its present condition. This is possibly the earliest known photograph of the mill, although no date is known for this picture.

A view of the Riddings windmills, Sarah and James. They were built in 1877 by James Oakes and named after himself and his wife. They ceased working in 1927 and were gutted by fire in January 1963; subsequently they were demolished.

One of the windmills after the fire, when it was being demolished.

Two views across the fields and quarry at Crich. In the distance, centre, can be seen one of the early Crich Stands.

There have been four landmarks on this site. The first was made of wood and was used for signalling when blasting at nearby Crich Quarry. It was replaced in 1788 by a conical stone tower. In turn, this was replaced in 1851 by the structure pictured to the left. This is already starting to crumble which is why a fourth stand was eventually needed. Below is the now familiar fourth memorial, Crich Stand, which was opened in 1923 as a memorial to the Sherwood Forester Regiment.

Crich Cross, which was obviously a meeting point for local children. This would not be possible today as it is now the central feature for the meeting of three busy, narrow roads.

The Old Vicarage at Town End, Crich. In the distance can be seen one of the early Crich stands.

The Nonconformist chapel at Pentrich. This dated back to 1666 but has now been demolished.

Part of the old bull ring cross which used to stand in the centre of the road in Pentrich. This was uncovered by accident in a wall. It was later replaced by a signpost combined with a lamp standard, which in turn has also now been removed following several road accidents.

SURROUNDING

VILLAGES

High Street, Codnor, c. 1928. Tram lines are visible down the middle of the road and the

trolley bus wires can be seen overhead.

Farnsworth's chemists on the corner of Mill Lane, Codnor, *c.* 1906.

Burton's off-licence situated on High Street, Codnor, *c.* 1910.

Kensit's shop, Mill Lane, Codnor, showing both an exterior shot and a close-up of the family. There is a stained glass window, in memory of the family, in Crosshill Church.

Children standing on the corner of Whitegates, Codnor, 1906.

This view of Nottingham Road in 1906 is reminiscent of days gone by. Not only can children no longer walk alone down a deserted street, but the road would now have traffic on it. Further down on the right, in the distance, can be seen the old French Horn pub.

A Salvation Army band performing outside the now demolished Drury Lowe Arms at Smithyhouses, Denby.

This thatched cottage stood on the left, near the traffic lights, at the corner of Yellow Yard, Swanwick. This photograph was taken in about 1915 and shows Mr and Mrs Beresford and their son, George. George later had a dance band in Ripley and was a well-known local pianist. He also kept a pub in Kilburn. His father was also musical, being a singer.

High Green, now known as Eagle Street, Heage, 1904. The small boy on the right is J. Stone when he was five years old. The building behind them is the White Hart. The wall has since been removed to allow for road widening.

Church Street, Heage, 1904. The small cottage on the right was demolished and Bowmer and Kirkland, a construction and plant hire firm, now have offices here. This road is much wider today.

Ridgeway Lane from Shawe or Butcher's Bank. The middle building was the Anchor inn, while on the right of it was the chapel, which has since been demolished.

The aqueduct at Sawmills, Ambergate, demolished in October 1968.

The old post office at Ambergate, *c.* 1900. This picture shows the mail being collected by horse-drawn carriage.

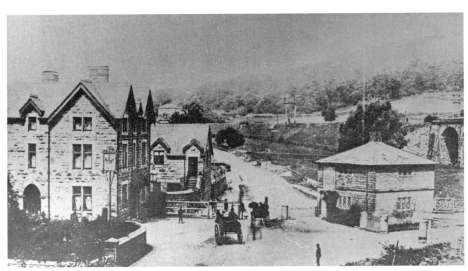

The Toll Bar near the Hurt Arms, Ambergate.

BRITAIN IN OLD PHOTOGRAPHS

To order any of these titles please telephone Littlehampton Book Services on 01903 721596

ALDERNEY

Alderney: A Second Selection, *B Bonnard*

BEDFORDSHIRE

Bedfordshire at Work, *N Lutt*

BERKSHIRE

Maidenhead, *M Hayles & D Hedges*
Around Maidenhead, *M Hayles & B Hedges*
Reading, *P Southerton*
Reading: A Second Selection, *P Southerton*
Sandhurst and Crowthorne, *K Dancy*
Around Slough, *J Hunter & K Hunter*
Around Thatcham, *P Allen*
Around Windsor, *B Hedges*

BUCKINGHAMSHIRE

Buckingham and District, *R Cook*
High Wycombe, *R Goodearl*
Around Stony Stratford, *A Lambert*

CHESHIRE

Cheshire Railways, *M Hitches*
Chester, *S Nichols*

CLWYD

Clwyd Railways, *M Hitches*

CLYDESDALE

Clydesdale, *Lesmahagow Parish Historical Association*

CORNWALL

Cornish Coast, *T Bowden*
Falmouth, *P Gilson*
Lower Fal, *P Gilson*
Around Padstow, *M McCarthy*
Around Penzance, *J Holmes*
Penzance and Newlyn, *J Holmes*
Around Truro, *A Lyne*
Upper Fal, *P Gilson*

CUMBERLAND

Cockermouth and District, *J Bernard Bradbury*
Keswick and the Central Lakes, *J Marsh*
Around Penrith, *F Boyd*
Around Whitehaven, *H Fancy*

DERBYSHIRE

Derby, *D Buxton*
Around Matlock, *D Barton*

DEVON

Colyton and Seaton, *T Gosling*
Dawlish and Teignmouth, *G Gosling*
Devon Aerodromes, *K Saunders*
Exeter, *P Thomas*
Exmouth and Budleigh Salterton, *T Gosling*
From Haldon to Mid-Dartmoor, *T Hall*
Honiton and the Otter Valley, *J Yallop*
Around Kingsbridge, *K Tanner*
Around Seaton and Sidmouth, *T Gosling*
Seaton, Axminster and Lyme Regis, *T Gosling*

DORSET

Around Blandford Forum, *B Cox*
Bournemouth, *M Colman*
Bridport and the Bride Valley, *J Burrell & S Humphries*
Dorchester, *T Gosling*
Around Gillingham, *P Crocker*

DURHAM

Darlington, *G Flynn*
Darlington: A Second Selection, *G Flynn*
Durham People, *M Richardson*
Houghton-le-Spring and Hetton-le-Hole, *K Richardson*
Houghton-le-Spring and Hetton-le-Hole:
    A Second Selection, *K Richardson*
Sunderland, *S Miller & B Bell*
Teesdale, *D Coggins*
Teesdale: A Second Selection, *P Raine*
Weardale, *J Crosby*
Weardale: A Second Selection, *J Crosby*

DYFED

Aberystwyth and North Ceredigion,
    Dyfed Cultural Services Dept
Haverfordwest, *Dyfed Cultural Services Dept*
Upper Tywi Valley, *Dyfed Cultural Services Dept*

ESSEX

Around Grays, *B Evans*

GLOUCESTERSHIRE

Along the Avon from Stratford to Tewkesbury, *J Jeremiah*
Cheltenham: A Second Selection, *R Whiting*
Cheltenham at War, *P Gill*
Cirencester, *J Welsford*
Around Cirencester, *E Cuss & P Griffiths*
Forest, The, *D Mullin*
Gloucester, *J Voyce*
Around Gloucester, *A Sutton*
Gloucester: From the Walwin Collection, *J Voyce*
North Cotswolds, *D Viner*
Severn Vale, *A Sutton*
Stonehouse to Painswick, *A Sutton*
Stroud and the Five Valleys, *S Gardiner & L Padin*
Stroud and the Five Valleys: A Second Selection,
    S Gardiner & L Padin
Stroud's Golden Valley, *S Gardiner & L Padin*
Stroudwater and Thames & Severn Canals,
    E Cuss & S Gardiner
Stroudwater and Thames & Severn Canals: A Second
    Selection, *E Cuss & S Gardiner*
Tewkesbury and the Vale of Gloucester, *C Hilton*
Thornbury to Berkeley, *J Hudson*
Uley, Dursley and Cam, *A Sutton*
Wotton-under-Edge to Chipping Sodbury, *A Sutton*

GWYNEDD

Anglesey, *M Hitches*
Gwynedd Railways, *M Hitches*
Around Llandudno, *M Hitches*
Vale of Conwy, *M Hitches*

HAMPSHIRE

Gosport, *J Sadden*
Portsmouth, *P Rogers & D Francis*

HEREFORDSHIRE

Herefordshire, *A Sandford*

HERTFORDSHIRE

Barnet, *I Norrie*
Hitchin, *A Fleck*
St Albans, *S Mullins*
Stevenage, *M Appleton*

ISLE OF MAN

The Tourist Trophy, *B Snelling*

ISLE OF WIGHT

Newport, *D Parr*
Around Ryde, *D Parr*

JERSEY

Jersey: A Third Selection, *R Lemprière*

KENT

Bexley, *M Scott*
Broadstairs and St Peter's, *J Whyman*
Bromley, Keston and Hayes, *M Scott*
Canterbury: A Second Selection, *D Butler*
Chatham and Gillingham, *P MacDougall*
Chatham Dockyard, *P MacDougall*
Deal, *J Broady*
Early Broadstairs and St Peter's, *B Wootton*
East Kent at War, *D Collyer*
Eltham, *J Kennett*
Folkestone: A Second Selection, *A Taylor & E Rooney*
Goudhurst to Tenterden, *A Guilmant*
Gravesend, *R Hiscock*
Around Gravesham, *R Hiscock & D Grierson*
Herne Bay, *J Hawkins*
Lympne Airport, *D Collyer*
Maidstone, *I Hales*
Margate, *R Clements*
RAF Hawkinge, *R Humphreys*
RAF Manston, *RAF Manston History Club*
RAF Manston: A Second Selection,
    RAF Manston History Club
Ramsgate and Thanet Life, *D Perkins*
Romney Marsh, *E Carpenter*
Sandwich, *C Wanostrocht*
Around Tonbridge, *C Bell*
Tunbridge Wells, *M Rowlands & I Beavis*
Tunbridge Wells: A Second Selection,
    M Rowlands & I Beavis
Around Whitstable, *C Court*
Wingham, Adisham and Littlebourne, *M Crane*

LANCASHIRE

Around Barrow-in-Furness, *J Garbutt & J Marsh*
Blackpool, *C Rothwell*
Bury, *J Hudson*
Chorley and District, *J Smith*
Fleetwood, *C Rothwell*
Heywood, *J Hudson*
Around Kirkham, *C Rothwell*
Lancashire North of the Sands, *J Garbutt & J Marsh*
Around Lancaster, *S Ashworth*
Lytham St Anne's, *C Rothwell*
North Fylde, *C Rothwell*
Radcliffe, *J Hudson*
Rossendale, *B Moore & N Dunnachie*

LEICESTERSHIRE

Around Ashby-de-la-Zouch, *K Hillier*
Charnwood Forest, *I Keil, W Humphrey & D Wix*
Leicester, *D Burton*
Leicester: A Second Selection, *D Burton*
Melton Mowbray, *T Hickman*
Around Melton Mowbray, *T Hickman*
River Soar, *D Wix, P Shacklock & I Keil*
Rutland, *J Clough*
Vale of Belvoir, *T Hickman*
Around the Welland Valley, *S Mastoris*

LINCOLNSHIRE

Grimsby, *J Tierney*
Around Grimsby, *J Tierney*
Grimsby Docks, *J Tierney*
Lincoln, *D Cuppleditch*